Lines o

West Highlands

IAN LOTHIAN

BRITAIN'S RAILWAYS SERIES, VOLUME 34

Front cover image: 66737 arriving at Rannoch on 7 March 2022, with the 08.07 empty Alumina tanks from Fort William to North Blyth.

Back cover image: 31190 and 37261 climb the last half mile to County March summit on 14 May 2005 with the 'Royal Scotsman' from Edinburgh on its way to Spean Bridge.

Title page image: 37503 and 37411 descending Glen Falloch between Crianlarich and Ardlui on 16 June 2000, with the then midday Fort William to Mossend freight.

Contents page image: 47854 passes County March on 28 August 2021 with a 15.10 Rannoch to Edinburgh 'Northern Belle', with 57314 on the rear.

Published by Key Books
An imprint of Key Publishing Ltd
PO Box 100
Stamford
Lincs PE19 1XQ

www.keypublishing.com

The right of Ian Lothian to be identified as the author of this book has been asserted in accordance with the Copyright, Designs and Patents Act 1988 Sections 77 and 78.

Copyright © Ian Lothian, 2022

ISBN 978 1 80282 350 9

Typeset by SJmagic DESIGN SERVICES, India.

Contents

Introduction

The lines from Glasgow Queen Street to Oban, Fort William and Mallaig are world famous for the scenery that they pass through. Once proposed for closure, they are now more dependent on the leisure market as the volume of freight carried has dwindled, with only the alumina traffic from North Blyth to the smelter at Fort William now remaining. The lines are signalled by Radio Electronic Token Block (RETB) controlled from the signalling centre at Banavie, and any train venturing past Helensburgh Upper has to have the appropriate equipment fitted in its cab. The RETB signalling was introduced in stages until it became fully operational in 1988.

I first travelled on these lines around 50 years ago and have done so on a regular basis ever since. When I first travelled, it was in a BR Mk.1 coach hauled by either a Class 24, 25 or 27 diesel. These locomotives then gave way to the Class 37s before they were in turn replaced by the Class 156 DMUs in early 1989 and they have worked all the passenger services since.

Two of Scotland's railway companies operated lines into the West Highlands, the Callander and Oban, which became part of the Caledonian Railway, running from Glasgow via Stirling, Callander and Crianlarich Lower to Oban and the North British Railway, whose line ran through the Glasgow suburbs and along the north bank of the Clyde to Craigendoran. Here, the line and the scenery changed from a built-up area to a rural setting with a single-track line that climbed past Helensburgh Upper, ran along firstly the Gairloch and then Loch Long before it reached Arrochar and Tarbet. It then ran along the west side of Loch Lomond to Ardlui, where it commenced the stiff climb up Glen Falloch to Crianlarich.

The original line to Oban via Callander, was built in stages between 1866 and 1880 with a spur line at Crianlarich that connected it to the West Highland Line. The line from Callander was closed in September 1965 due to a rockslide in Glen Ogle. It had been proposed to close this section that November; the rock fall merely brought the closure date forward.

Between Crianlarich and Tyndrum, both lines go their own way, the Oban line runs along the western side of the valley floor to Tyndrum Lower, after which it passes through Glen Lochy to Dalmally and after running alongside Loch Awe and negotiating the Pass of Brander, it arrives at Taynuilt on Loch Etive. It then runs along Loch Etive to Connel Ferry, once the junction of a branch line to Ballachuilish, before turning inland, climbing over Glencruitten Summit and descending to the station beside the ferry terminal at Oban.

The line to Fort William leaves Crianlarich, and after crossing over the road and the site of the former Callander and Oban line, it crosses the River Dochart and curves to start the climb to Upper Tyndrum and the summit at County March. It then descends around the Horseshoe Bend and runs along the base of Beinn Dorain to Bridge of Orchy. It then starts to climb up onto the desolate Rannoch Moor, passing Rannoch station and continuing to climb until it reaches the summit at Corrour, 1,350ft above sea level. After the summit, the line descends steeply alongside Loch Treig to reach Tulloch, and it then runs west passing the hamlet of Roy Bridge then Spean Bridge before arriving at Fort William. This line has several times been voted the most scenic railway journey in the world.

At Fort William Junction, the Mallaig extension starts its journey to the west coast, this being one of the last major rail construction projects, as it was only opened in 1901, but it allowed Mallaig to become an important fishing port. Nowadays, the line is famous for 'The Jacobite' steam service, which runs from Easter until November. Glenfinnan Viaduct has become world famous since appearing in the Harry Potter films, which in turn gave the line a much-needed publicity boost.

I have photographed trains on these lines for many years, my only regret is that I never ventured out onto Rannoch Moor when I was both younger and able to do so. I have a substantial collection of photographs from locations that are both scenic and easily accessed and I hope that you will enjoy this book. It is a collection of both old and recent photographs showing a variety of motive power and liveries.

I have to thank Key Publishing for the opportunity to produce this book. Especially, I must thank my family – Christopher and Laura had to wait at times while dad photographed a train, often in the middle of nowhere! Special thanks, as always, go to my wife, Irene; without her help, this book would have remained a dream and would never have become a reality.

Ian Lothian
Larbert, 2022

37428 crosses the Awe Viaduct on 11 May 2003 with the Royal Scotsman from Taynuilt to Arrochar.

Chapter 1

Glasgow Queen Street to Helensburgh

Our Journey to the West Highlands will start in the middle of Scotland's largest city, Glasgow, and will run through what was once a highly industrialised area before passing through the outer Glasgow suburbs and eventually reaching the north bank of the River Clyde, which it will then follow as far as the junction at Craigendoran. The electrified line that West Highland Line trains have used from Westerton runs close to the Clyde Estuary to its terminus at Helensburgh Central, while the West Highland Line starts a stiff climb on single track to Helensburgh Upper.

Glasgow Queen Street is the terminus that was first built by the Edinburgh and Glasgow Railway and opened in 1842. It was originally called Dundas Street station, but this was changed to Queen Street shortly afterwards. It was built on the site of a former quarry, and the original plan of the Edinburgh and Glasgow Railway was to have its terminus at a higher elevation to the north of its present site. This would have involved the railway crossing over the Forth and Clyde Canal on a bridge, but opposition by the canal company resulted in the railway having to descend from Cowlairs to Queen Street on a gradient of 1 in 42 so as to pass under the canal in a tunnel before emerging into the station.

Due to the steep gradient, trains were hauled up the incline by a wire rope with a winding engine built at the top at Cowlairs, which was used until 1909. The steep climb out of the station resulted in an accident in 1928 when a passenger service stalled on the hill and ran backwards, colliding with another train at the station and resulting in three people being killed and more badly injured.

The closure of the former Caledonian Railway station at Buchanan Street in 1966 resulted in Queen Street's rather cramped layout, which has only six long platforms as platform one is short and only able to be used by local suburban services, becoming busier which often caused delays. Queen Street has two low-level platforms used by the Glasgow north-side electric suburban services and, after the reopening of the Bathgate to Airdrie line, by through services between Edinburgh Waverley and Helensburgh Central.

Queen Street has been rebuilt several times over the years; the most noticeable improvement being the rebuilding for the electrification of the line to Edinburgh with the lengthening of platforms two to five to be able to hold eight-coach electric trains. A new concourse and frontage completed the rebuilding and also allowed a view of the station's overall roof, built in 1878, from George Square.

Several of the trains using the West Highland Line have both a portion for Oban and for Fort William and Mallaig with these services dividing at Crianlarich and with some southbound services also combining there for the remainder of their journey to Glasgow. All trains are formed of Class 156 DMUs; these units have worked all West Highland services since their introduction in 1989. West Highland services carry a large number of leisure passengers and transporting bicycles and rucksacks in a DMU with limited luggage space was a problem.

A solution was the acquisition by ScotRail of five single-car Class 153 DMUs, which were converted by Brodie Engineering at Kilmarnock with half the original seating removed and that space fitted out to carry up to 20 cycles and also having room for rucksacks. The Class 153s have seating for up to 20 passengers, although a premium fare is charged to travel in them. Although this seems expensive, passengers travelling in them receive a free cup of tea or coffee and a bag containing a bottle of water, ploughman's lunch sandwiches and some shortbread biscuits, making the cost of the travel premium a lot more reasonable!

After climbing Cowlairs Incline, trains pass the site of where the North British Railway, then the London and North Eastern Railway (LNER) and subsequently British Railways had a major engine and rolling stock building and repair works, but nothing now remains of what was once a huge industrial complex. The line branches off the route to Edinburgh and curves sharply round to Cowlairs North Junction before starting to run westwards towards Maryhill on a line built by the Glasgow, Dumbarton and Helensburgh Railway, later absorbed into the North British Railway. Local services on this line were withdrawn in the 1960s, but then five new stations were opened in 1993 to improve travel in the north of Glasgow and the line passes through the first one at Ashfield, shortly after passing Cowlairs North junction. At Maryhill, a line reopened in 2005 runs to Anniesland with an intermediate station at Kelvindale.

At Knightswood North Junction, trains to the West Highlands join the electrified line from Queen Street Low Level, and after passing Westerton, trains soon arrive at Dalmuir, the first stop for West Highland Line services. After Dalmuir, trains start to run along the north bank of the River Clyde, passing under the Erskine Road Bridge and the stations at Kilpatrick and Bowling before arriving at Dumbarton Central, the next stop for West Highland services. The distance from Dumbarton Central to the next station at Dalreoch is less than a mile but involves crossing the River Leven, and the building of this bridge meant that it was a year after it had arrived at Dumbarton before the railway reached Dalreoch, the junction of the line to Balloch, which leaves the line to Helensburgh at the west end of the station.

The four-mile-long line to Balloch is now mostly single track, and the line terminates at a single platform station that was opened in 1988. There are two intermediate stations at Renton and Alexandria and the journey time from Dalreoch with the two stops is only nine minutes. The new Balloch station replaced the former Balloch Central station, which was a two-platform station on the west side of Balloch Road. This had a level crossing that caused frequent delays to road traffic at busy times. The line originally continued to Balloch Pier where it connected with sailings by the *Maid of the Loch* passenger boat. *Maid of the Loch* ceased services on Loch Lomond in 1981, although it is now being restored to work again, and the line from Balloch Central to Balloch Pier closed in 1986. An interesting fact is that the present Balloch station lies just over 150 metres inside the Loch Lomond and Trossachs National Park and is the only overhead electrified railway in any national park in the UK.

After leaving Dalreoch, trains for Helensburgh and the West Highland Line curve to the southwest and pass through the two single-bore Dalreoch Tunnels. This section of the line has seen recent flooding, causing the line to be temporarily closed during recent periods of very heavy rain. The line then runs alongside the Clyde estuary providing good views for passengers as the line approaches the station at Cardross. After passing through Cardross, the line soon approaches Craigendoran Junction where the electrified line continues west to a station at Craigendoran before terminating at the three-platform Helensburgh Central station. The line from Craigendoran Junction to Helensburgh Central is now just single track. Helensburgh Central was opened in 1858 but was completely rebuilt in 1897 by the engineer James Carswell, better known for designing the overall roof at Queen Street station and the two approach viaducts at the Forth Bridge. The station commands a very central location in the town and before the Covid pandemic was used on average by around 750,000 passengers a year.

Craigendoran Junction is the real start of the West Highland Line; it now becomes a single-track line and starts to climb up to the first station for northbound services at Helensburgh Upper. This used to be a typical West Highland station with an island platform and the ability for trains running in opposite directions to pass, but the line on the north side of the platform was removed in 1968. With a very sparse service and long gaps between trains, it is not surprising to find that Helensburgh Upper is only used by just under 15,000 passengers each year. There is also a noticeable change as our journey commenced in a heavily built-up area followed by miles of suburbia, but by the time we have left Dalreoch it was running through open countryside. Helensburgh is the last town the line encounters until reaching either Oban or Fort William.

Above: 153377 and 156492 wait at Glasgow Queen Street on 25 August 2021 with the 10.34 to Oban.

Left: 153370 and 156457 depart from Glasgow Queen Street with the 10.34 to Oban on 18 August 2021, passing 385010, which had arrived on a service from Alloa.

The only regular freight working on the West Highland lines is the flow of alumina north to Fort William and the southbound empty tanks to North Blyth. 66737, a regular locomotive on these workings, is approaching Cowlairs North Junction with loaded tanks for Fort William on 5 April 2016.

The southbound empty alumina tanks are behind 66740 between Ashfield and Cowlairs North Junction on 9 May 2016.

Several trains to and from Oban, Fort William and Mallaig either divide or join at Crianlarich. On 22 April 2022, the 10.10 from Mallaig and the 12.11 from Oban joined at Crianlarich, and, with 156499 leading 156453 and 156445, the three Class 156s are between Ashfield and Cowlairs North Junction on the last part of their journey to Glasgow Queen Street.

156458 is arriving at Dalmuir on 17 February 2022, the last stop before Glasgow Queen Street for the 06.03 from Mallaig. 320401 was working the 10.14 from Airdrie to Balloch.

153305, one of the five Class 153s converted to carry bicycles and luggage as well as having seats for 20 passengers, has 156445 behind it as the 10.34 from Glasgow Queen Street to Oban stops at Dumbarton Central on 21 February 2022.

Trains heading for the West Highlands run along the North Clyde electric line for the first part of their journey. On 5 March 2022, 334009 with 334019 behind calls at Dumbarton Central with the 13.08 from Edinburgh Waverley to Helensburgh Central.

A rare visitor to Dumbarton Central on 5 March 2022 was 'The Statesman', a Pullman train hauled by a pair of Class 47s with 47614 leading 47593 and working a 05.56 Stevenage to Fort William excursion.

The converted Class 153s have certainly brought a splash of colour to the railway. On 26 August 2021, 153373 is coupled behind 156474 on the 14.41 from Oban to Glasgow Queen Street as they cross the River Leven and are about to arrive at Dumbarton Central.

Every year since they were introduced on the Fort William to Mallaig line in 1984, steam trains have run in the West Highlands. To take the steam locomotive and coaches north, a diesel loco is often used to haul the train when there has been a period of dry weather, so as to reduce the risk of lineside fires. On 16 June 2000, the unusual combination of Fragonset Class 31 31190 and BR Standard Class 4 75014 are seen as they cross the Leven Viaduct going to Fort William.

On a bitterly cold 30 March 2022, the 04.26 Carnforth to Fort William empty stock for 'The Jacobite' steam service on the Mallaig line is seen as it crosses the Leven Viaduct. 37516 had failed at Dalmuir and was being pushed by Black Five 45407 and another Black Five, 44871, which was on the rear of the train. The two steam engines powered the train to the loop at Craigendoran where they had to wait for just over seven hours for a replacement Class 37 to arrive to take the train north to Fort William.

Class 66s were given clearance to run over the West Highland Line, and EWS then started to use one on the North Blyth to Fort William alumina tanks instead of a Class 37. On 3 May 2004, 66114 crossed the Leven Viaduct with the loaded tanks to Fort William.

156500 crosses the Leven Viaduct on 30 March 2022 with the 08.57 Oban to Glasgow Queen Street.

320411 and 318253 cross the Leven Viaduct and are about to enter Dalreoch station, less than a mile from Dumbarton Central on the east side of the river. The pair were working the 12.44 from Airdrie to Balloch.

Dalreoch is the junction for the lines to Balloch and Craigendoran, where the West Highland Line leaves the electrified line that terminates at Helensburgh Central. 156450 is negotiating the sharply curved line into Dalreoch on 21 February 2022 with the 10.14 Crianlarich to Glasgow Queen Street, which should have started at Oban but due to an operational problem had begun its journey at Crianlarich.

Running a mere five minutes behind the Class 156 was the 11.25 Helensburgh Central to Edinburgh Waverley, formed of 334021 and 334024. This shows how tightly curved parts of this line are.

The line to Balloch is now just a single track from a short distance after the line leaves Dalreoch. At the new Balloch station, opened in 1988, 318253 and 320411 will shortly depart with the 14.08 to Airdrie on 5 March 2022.

On 23 April 1984, 314208 waits at the former Balloch Central station with the 17.40 to Motherwell. In the distance, a Class 311 EMU has just departed on the short run to the station at Balloch Pier.

After Dalreoch, the line runs along the northern side of the Clyde estuary and on 4 March 2000, Deltic 55019 was approaching Cardross with a Cardiff to Fort William 'Monarch of the Glen' railtour, which it worked from Motherwell.

320305 in the original Strathclyde PTE orange livery is seen at Cardross on 4 March 2000 with the 16.15 Helensburgh Central to Airdrie.

334032 arrives at Cardross on 30 December 2002 in the revised carmine and cream SPT livery with the 10.54 from Helensburgh to Airdrie.

Some 21 years later, the Class 334s are still working all the services that now stop at Cardross. On 5 March 2022, 334036 and 334008 arrive at Cardross with the 12.55 from Helensburgh Central to Edinburgh Waverley.

At Craigendoran junction, just east of Helensburgh, the West Highland Line leaves the North Clyde electrified line and becomes a single-track railway and climbs towards Helensburgh Upper. The electrified line terminates at Helensburgh Central, where 334006 and 334025 are waiting to depart with the 11.52 to Edinburgh Waverley on 5 March 2022.

Chapter 2

Helensburgh to Crianlarich

Helensburgh Upper was opened on 7 August 1894, when the line to Fort William was opened to through traffic, and it is located up a hill from the town centre in a residential area. In typical West Highland style, it was an island platform with the station buildings and signal box on the platform. During World War Two, to cope with a vast increase in traffic especially to the military port at Faslane, the loops were extended westwards, and a new signal box was built. The former up platform was taken out of use in 1968 and the platform widened. The original station buildings and signal box were demolished and the only facility that it now has is a very basic waiting shelter.

The west end of the station platform is where the RETB signalling starts, and this is controlled from one of two panels in the signalling centre at Banavie. With less than 10,000 passengers using it every year and only six ScotRail services in each direction plus the two Caledonian Sleeper services, one each way between Fort William and London Euston, there are times every day when it can be a very quiet station.

After calling at Helensburgh Upper and being given the token to proceed, trains depart for Garelochhead, the next station that is still open. The line has now started to run through very rural surroundings and soon passes the site of the former station at Rhu. This was opened at the same time that the line was opened, 7 August 1894, and was originally called Row. Unusually for a station at the southern end of the West Highland Line, instead of the usual island platform, Row was a two platform station and for many years had a camping coach in an adjacent siding. In 1927, the station name was changed from Row to Rhu.

As well as the usual six trains each way plus the sleepers, Rhu was also served by the Arrochar and Tarbet to Craigendoran push-pull local service, latterly worked by a diesel railbus. The station was closed in 1956 but was reopened in 1960 before finally being closed again on 15 June 1964, and the buildings were demolished shortly after closure.

The line now runs westwards on the hillside above the Gairloch and in 1945, a station was built there and called Faslane Platform. Its primary task was to transport prisoners of war from two nearby POW camps to the temporary stations built in Glen Falloch, north of Ardlui, where they worked on the construction of the Loch Sloy hydro-electric scheme until the station was taken out of use in 1949.

The next original station on the line was at Shandon, which was opened in 1894. It had the usual island platform with a crossing loop but was closed on 15 June 1964. The signal box and loop survived until the beginning of April 1967, after which all the buildings and the platform were totally removed, and the single running line was realigned to run through where the middle of the platform had once been. As a result, there is very little evidence to be seen of the former station.

The line shortly reaches the site of the junction where the Faslane Military Railway branched off the West Highland Line and descended steeply to the dockside of what was then called Military Port No.1. Apart from the first couple of hundred yards, it was built as a double track line with right-hand running to train military crews for what they would encounter in mainland Europe. As it descended to the port, it crossed the road that led to Shandon station and then crossed the A814 road on a level crossing operated by a signal box.

In April 1946, Faslane ceased to be a military port and operation of the line was taken over by the LNER, although the line was still owned by the Ministry of Defence. The line was singled in May 1946, and its final use was to serve a ship-breaking site at the port, after which it was closed, and the tracks were lifted.

The next station and one that is still open today is Garelochhead, which is a typical West Highland island platform with the station buildings and signal box situated on the platform and passenger access being by means of a subway and steps. On 15 February 1987, in connection with the introduction of the RETB signalling, right hand running was introduced to make access to the sidings easier following the introduction of spring-loaded points that controlled access to the station. This meant that the former down platform became the new up platform while the former up platform is now the present day down platform.

After Garelochhead, the line soon passes the site of Whistlefield station, a minor station with only a single platform, which was opened in 1896 to serve a local estate. Like Shandon, it was also used to transport prisoners of war to the construction sites on the Loch Sloy hydro-electric project. In 1960, it was renamed Whistlefield Halt and finally closed in 1964 when the local service from Arrochar and Tarbet to Craigendoran was withdrawn.

The line continues westwards and climbs until it reaches the summit at Glen Douglas, 560ft above sea level. Glen Douglas had a private platform from 1926 until 1961, when it was opened to the public until, like other local stations, it was closed as from 15 June 1964. Glen Douglas had the usual West Highland island platform with a station building and a tall brick signal box at its eastern end but all of these have since been demolished. The Ministry of Defence depot at Glen Douglas is still rail connected and still sees occasional use.

After passing Glen Douglas, the line soon runs along a ledge in the hillside high above Loch Long, which it follows almost to the next station at Arrochar and Tarbet. The station is situated between the two villages that give it its name, Arrochar at the head of Loch Long and Tarbet on Loch Lomond. The station used to have camping coaches until all such vehicles were withdrawn from use in 1969. Timber was loaded here until 2008 when the traffic was halted due to the economic recession, but it has never restarted.

A run north along the west bank of Loch Lomond, Scotland's largest loch, takes the line to Ardlui, situated at the head of the loch. There used to be some excellent views of the loch along this part of the line but there are places now where only an occasional glimpse can be had due to the unchecked growth of lineside vegetation. An attempt has been made to clear small areas, but much more needs to be done. As the line runs along the side of Loch Lomond, it passes the site of the former station at Inveruglas that was opened in 1945 as a private station and closed in 1948, being used by the former prisoners of war who were employed on the Loch Sloy hydro-electric scheme and brought to Inveruglas from the stations at Shandon and Whistlefield.

Due to subsidence, the station buildings at Ardlui had to be demolished, and there is now just a waiting shelter and the former signal box at the northern end of the platform remaining. In January 1986, the semaphore signalling was removed, and, after trials, the RETB signalling became fully operational at the end of March 1986. In February 1987, the running lines were altered to right hand running to allow easy access to what are now engineers' sidings on the east side of the line at the north end of the station.

The line leaves Ardlui and immediately starts a gruelling climb up Glen Falloch. In connection with the Loch Sloy hydro-electric scheme, there was another temporary station, which was called

Glen Falloch Halt, opened in 1946 and closed towards the end of 1948. The line continues climbing until it reaches a level and then slightly downhill section before arriving at Crianlarich. This was nicknamed 'The Fireman's Rest' in steam day's as it was the only break a fireman had from continuously shovelling coal on a line that climbed virtually all the way from Ardlui to County March Summit.

The line soon reaches Crianlarich station, which was opened on 7 August 1894. The land that the station, turntable, engine shed and sidings were built on was the subject of a government compulsory purchase as the local landowner would not agree to the construction of the line across his land as he stated that it would interfere with his ability to shoot game. The spur line to join the Caledonian line from Callander to Oban was built in 1897. The station buildings were destroyed by fire in 1937 but were rebuilt and include the tearoom that is still open today.

The Caledonian line had reached Crianlarich Lower at the beginning of August 1873, 21 years before the arrival of the West Highland Line, and until its station was closed in 1965, this small village with a population of around 200 people was served by two stations on two different lines! The engine shed still remains; it is classed as a Group C listed building and is now used by the permanent way engineering staff.

Left: 153377 and 156500 wait time at Helensburgh Upper on 5 March 2022 with the 10.34 from Glasgow Queen Street to Oban.

Below: 156474 is approaching Helensburgh Upper on 5 March 2022 with the 08.57 from Oban to Glasgow Queen Street, on track that could do with the visit of a weedkiller train.

The line west of Helensburgh Upper starts to run through some very rural countryside. On 5 March 2022, 156476 approaches Helensburgh Upper with the 06.03 from Mallaig to Glasgow Queen Street.

Making its first ever appearance on the North Blyth to Fort William alumina tanks, Royal Scotsman-liveried 66746 approaches Garelochhead on 31 March 2022.

Garelochhead is one of several stations on the West Highland Line that have right hand running due to the RETB signalling's spring-operated points requiring this change in order for trains to easily access the sidings at Garelochhead. 156450 is arriving with the combined 10.10 from Mallaig and the 12.11 from Oban on 30 March 2022.

153373 leads 156456 into Garelochhead on 25 August 2021 with the 16.36 from Glasgow Queen Street to Oban.

37606 waits at Arrochar & Tarbet on 5 April 2000 to receive the token for the single line to Garelochhead with the Freightliner-operated Fort William to Coatbridge, this conveying aluminium ingots.

153377 and 156492 wait at Arrochar & Tarbet for a bicycle to be unloaded on 25 August 2021 while working the 10.34 from Glasgow Queen Street to Oban.

66737 climbs up to Arrochar & Tarbet on 21 April 2022 with the 06.25 North Blyth to Fort William alumina tanks.

The Class 156 'Super Sprinters' took over the West Highland passenger services in 1989, and on 16 June 2000, 156476 and 156485 arrived at Ardlui having joined together at Crianlarich; 156476 having started at Fort William and 156485 at Oban.

37406 in EWS maroon livery coasts through Ardlui running long section from Crianlarich to Arrochar & Tarbet with an engineers' train returning to Mossend on 8 June 2006.

On 12 June 2021, a pair of Locomotive Services Class 37s in BR green and carrying their original numbers of D6817 and D6851 passed through Ardlui with a long section token from Crianlarich to Arrochar & Tarbet with a 13.50 private charter from Oban to Crewe.

37413 and 37419 run downgrade in Glen Falloch on 5 April 2000 with the afternoon Fort William to Mossend freight.

Also photographed on 5 April 2000 was the Fort William to Coatbridge Freightliner service, which carried the aluminium ingots, photographed as it ran south down Glen Falloch behind 37606.

The weather is not always dry and sunny in the West Highlands. Despite a promising weather forecast, when Deltic 55019 ran south on 5 March 2000, it had turned into a day of torrential rain and poor visibility, but it was still worth capturing such a rare event.

The weather conditions on 5 May 2008 were ideal when 37248 and 37688 ran down Glen Falloch with a railtour returning from Oban to Newcastle.

The Royal train runs south in Glen Falloch as 47798, with 47799 on the rear, goes slowly towards Ardlui on 9 November 2002 with the empty stock returning to Wolverton from Spean Bridge.

50049 ran down Glen Falloch on a very cold but clear and bright 6 March 2005 with a 'Monarch of the Glen' railtour returning south from Fort William with 50031 on the rear.

After reaching the summit of the climb up Glen Falloch, the line runs on a slight downhill gradient to Crianlarich, known in steam days as 'The Fireman's Rest' as it was the only part of the journey north to Fort William until County March Summit was reached where a fireman could have a short rest from shovelling coal into the firebox. On 21 April 2022, 66737 runs towards Crianlarich with the 06.25 North Blyth to Fort William loaded alumina tanks.

The most unusual sight of a pair of 'Dutch'-liveried Class 31s on a railtour returning south from Fort William occurred on 3 August 1996 when 31146 and 31166 left Crianlarich on their way south.

Before the use of a Class 66 on the Alcan tanks, it was a shorter train hauled by a Class 37 that ran more frequently. On 16 June 2000, 37419 leaves Crianlarich with empty tanks for North Blyth.

A pair of Class 156s, in the then new National Express ScotRail livery, leave Crianlarich for Glasgow Queen Street on 22 May 2004.

On a very wet
5 September 1987,
37408 waits at
Crianlarich with a Fort
William to Glasgow
Queen Street service
as 37405 arrives with
a train from Glasgow
to Oban.

156492 leads a train
from Glasgow Queen
Street into Crianlarich
on 20 July 2021.
146492 will then run
to Oban while 156446,
and 156478 will depart
soon afterwards for
Fort William and
Mallaig.

31190 in Royal
Scotsman maroon
leads Fragonset black
31602 into Crianlarich
from Fort William with
the 'Royal Scotsman'
on 29 May 2005 on its
way to Taynuilt on the
Oban line.

The first appearance by a Class 67 on sleeper coaches was on 4 October 2003 when 67004 worked a trial from Polmadie to Fort William and back. 67004 is seen as it arrives at Crianlarich on its way north to Fort William.

66105 arrives at Crianlarich with the North Blyth to Fort William loaded alumina tanks on 3 May 2008.

In the mid-1980s, an Oban to Grangemouth empty fuel tank working was having a wagon examined at Crianlarich before 37011 was able to continue its journey south.

156456 waits at Crianlarich on the beautifully sunny morning of 1 September 2021 with the 08.57 Oban to Glasgow Queen Street as 156477 leading 156493 and 156474 had just arrived from Glasgow. 156477 was detached and then departed to Oban while the other two formed a service to Fort William and Mallaig.

Chapter 3
Crianlarich to Oban

The line from Crianlarich to Oban was part of the Callander and Oban Railway (C&O), which was built in stages between 1866 and 1880. The aim of the line was to link the port of Oban on the west coast of Scotland to industrial Central Scotland. The problems that the C&O faced were having to build a line over 70 miles long through some very mountainous country with no major towns on its proposed route that would generate much-needed income and having to raise the capital required to pay for the line's construction. Lack of money was the reason it took so long to build and why it had to be built in stages.

By the beginning of June 1870, the line from Callander had reached a temporary terminus at Glen Oglehead. The railway was then extended from there to Tyndrum, and the station at Crianlarich was opened on 1 August 1873 with the line terminating at a station with an engine shed at Tyndrum. On 11 July 1874, Royal Assent was given for the construction of the line from Tyndrum to Oban, and the next section to be built was to Dalmally at the head of Loch Awe with that line opening on 1 May 1877, and then finally the section from Dalmally to Oban was completed and the line through to Oban opened on 30 June 1880.

Crianlarich station had two platforms with a signal box and sidings and trains going in opposite directions were able to pass there. After the West Highland Line had reached its station in Crianlarich in 1894, a spur line connecting it with the line to Oban was built in 1897, and a loop was built at the new junction. After World War One, the loop at the station was taken out of use in 1921 and the northern platform subsequently demolished. In 1951 the two stations were renamed, the one on the Oban line became Crianlarich Lower while the West Highland station became Crianlarich Upper.

By the early 1960s, it was obvious that traffic was declining and to reduce costs, it was proposed that the line between Callander, and the junction where the line from the West Highland joined the Oban line to the west of Crianlarich would be closed. A closure date of 1 November 1965 was decided on, but a major rockfall in Glen Ogle caused the line to close on 28 September 1965 with trains between Glasgow and Oban now using the West Highland Line as far as Crianlarich Upper, which was then renamed Crianlarich. The former Lower station and its goods yard remained in use for loading timber, and a loop line was reinstated there so that the locomotives on the timber trains could run round. The timber traffic was transferred to the upper yard from 1993, enabling the tracks to be lifted and the station site is now lost beneath the local community centre with housing having been built on the former goods yard.

After leaving Crianlarich, the line to Oban has a five mile run up Strathfillan before arriving at the village of Tyndrum. This was the terminus of the line from 1873 until 1877, and the original station had a platform and a small engine shed with some sidings for goods traffic. When it was decided to extend the line to Dalmally, a new alignment had to be made and a new station at Tyndrum was built about 300 yards to the west of the original terminus and at a higher elevation as the new line had to climb to cross the saddle of land just over half a mile to the west that divides Strathfillan from Glen Lochy. The new station had two platforms with a passing loop and a signal box. The former terminus became the goods yard and after that closed, the land is now used as a holiday caravan park. In 1969, as part of a cost cutting and rationalisation plan, the western platform and the crossing loop were taken out of use and the signal box was closed.

To differentiate between the two stations in Tyndrum, in 1992 the one on the Oban line was named Tyndrum Lower, while the station on the West Highland Line to Fort William was named Upper Tyndrum. In 1988, Tyndrum Lower became a token exchange point for the new RETB signalling. At the last census, Tyndrum had a resident population of just under 170 and yet enjoys the luxury of having two stations on two different railway lines and is the smallest village in the UK to have two open stations. As it is a very popular holiday and recreational area, around 5,500 people use Tyndrum Lower station in a year with around 5,000 using Upper Tyndrum!

After leaving Tyndrum Lower, the line climbs steeply to the summit just over half a mile to the west, after which it starts to run down Glen Lochy towards the next station at Dalmally. This part of the line shows the difficulty and cost that faced its construction and operation. Tyndrum has an elevation of 1,178 feet above sea level while Dalmally, 12 miles to the west, is only 296 feet above sea level so eastbound trains face a stiff climb up Glen Lochy on their way to Tyndrum.

Dalmally has a resident population of just over 550 and with no villages between Tyndrum and Dalmally, it also illustrates what little intermediate traffic there was along the line. In recent years, due to the availability of holiday accommodation and it being an area popular with walkers, the number of passengers using Dalmally has increased and despite the Covid outbreak, the latest figures show an annual usage of nearly 13,000 with the majority of these journeys being made in the summer months. Dalmally also has a daily school train to Oban in the morning and a return service in the late afternoon. The station has two platforms and while the platform for trains to Oban only has a basic waiting shelter, the up platform has a substantial station building with a canopy and the former signal box, both of which are category B listed buildings. As elsewhere, the signals were all removed on 9 February 1986 as part of the preparation for the introduction of the RETB signalling, which was commissioned in March 1988. When the line reached Dalmally and was opened on 1 April 1877, it was for the next three years the western terminus of the line so, for a short while, there was an engine shed and turntable on the south side of the line. The route on to Oban was finally opened to traffic on 1 July 1880.

While Glen Lochy can be described as fairly bleak, the scenery after Dalmally is stunning. Just over a mile to the west, the line crosses the recently renovated Awe Viaduct and curves to the west to run alongside Loch Awe, Scotland's longest loch. Good views can be had of Kilchurn Castle, one of four castles in the Dalmally area. This was built in the mid-1400s by Sir Colin Campbell, but it was abandoned in the mid-1700s. It is owned by Historic Scotland and is open to the public. After a short run, trains for Oban then arrive at Loch Awe station, serving the village of Lochawe. Although the village only has a resident population of just over 200, it has a large number of holiday accommodations and is also popular with walkers and the station has an annual usage of just over 5,000. It is a single platform station with just a waiting shelter and is on the north side (the village side) of the line.

After leaving Loch Awe, the line runs along a shelf cut out of the hillside with good views of the loch. After three-and-a-half miles, the line reaches the platform at Falls of Cruachan. This small station has just a basic waiting shelter and was first opened on 1 October 1893. It is situated at the base of Ben Cruachan, 3,694ft in height, so the station is popular with hill walkers. As an economy measure, it was closed on 1 November 1965 but then reopened on 20 June 1988. It is only open each year between March and the end of October, but in that time, it is used by around 1,000 people.

The next station after Falls of Cruachan is Taynuilt, six and a half miles to the west. Firstly though, the railway runs through the Pass of Brander where the railway and the adjacent main road have to squeeze between the base of Ben Cruachan and Loch Awe. In 1881, a train hit rocks that had fallen from the mountainside and the then-Secretary of the Callander and Oban Railway, John Anderson, devised a series of horizontal wires connected to 17 special signals. Each one apart from the two end ones (Nos. 1 and 17) have two signal arms, one for each direction. If rocks fall, hitting and breaking a wire, the signals go to danger to stop the next train that comes along. The length of line covered by these signals is just under four miles in length, and when the wind blows and passes through the wires, it makes a musical noise, and the wires are known as 'Anderson's Piano'. Despite the presence of the wires, there have been two further accidents, in1946 a rock fall coincided with the passing of a train and in 2010, when a rock fall occurred on the railway side of the wires and derailed a Class 156. In 2021, this part of the line was awarded a 'Red Wheels Plaque' by the National Transport Trust in recognition of it being a site of historical importance to transport heritage.

The line then descends towards Taynuilt, a large village with a population of just over 800 and well frequented by visitors, being used in the last year by 35,000 passengers. The station is a two-platform affair with a passing loop. On 11 January 1987, it was altered to right hand running so that the former up platform became the new down platform with the former down platform now the new up platform. This was done so that shunting moves in or out of the sidings did not have to handpump the spring-loaded points that were introduced with the RETB signalling. The signal box closed on 27 March 1988 when the RETB signalling was introduced through to Oban and then relocated at the north end of the present up platform to serve as a waiting shelter for a time. As Taynuilt is only 62ft above sea level, it marks the start of a long climb for trains going to Crianlarich.

The line leaves Taynuilt and runs south on the east side of Loch Etive for the next seven miles to Connel, originally called Connel Ferry. In 1903, a branch line was built from Connel Ferry to Ballachuilish, but this line was closed in 1966. The most noticeable feature in Connel is the cantilever bridge that used to carry the branch line over the Falls of Lora at the west end of Loch Etive, now used by road traffic. When the line opened in 1880, Connel had two platforms and a passing loop. After the branch was built, an additional platform with a bay was built as was a turntable to the east of the line that was used to turn the branch locomotive. After the branch closed, the former island platform was abandoned and demolished. In 1968, an oil storage depot was opened but this is no longer served by rail and its tracks have all been lifted. Connel is a token exchange point for the RETB signalling.

After leaving Connel, the line turns away from Loch Etive and climbs for three miles to Glen Cruitten summit at just over 300ft above sea level and then starts a steep curving descent over the remaining three miles to arrive at Oban. The town is a major ferry terminal with the station situated alongside. When the station was built, it had two platforms, one and two, under an overall roof. In 1904, two additional platforms were built, three and four, which were situated closer to the ferry terminal. The trainshed roof over platforms one and two was sadly allowed to fall into disrepair and these two platforms were taken out of use in 1982 and, despite it being a listed building, was subsequently demolished. A new station building was constructed in 1986 beside the two remaining platforms, which are still numbered three and four!

Oban has a population of approximately 8,500 and with ferries running to the islands of Lismore, Colonsay, Islay, Coll and Tiree and to Craignure on Mull, Castlebay on Barra and at certain times of the year to Lochboisdale on South Uist, it is no surprise that Oban is Calmac's busiest ferry terminal. Train travel over the West Highland and Oban lines is not quick, as most of the journey is on a single track line with trains frequently having to wait at crossing places if there is any late running. Oban to Glasgow by rail is 101.3 miles but the average journey time is around three and a quarter hours. Despite this, Oban station is used by around 175,000 passengers each year. The pandemic and travel restrictions saw a marked drop in usage, but numbers are once again increasing towards pre-Covid levels.

The signalling at the west end of Crianlarich is operated by the driver, who has to select the route and contact Banavie signalling centre for permission to proceed, and only when that has been given will he be signalled to depart.

31190 and 31602 depart from Crianlarich on their way to Taynuilt with the 'Royal Scotsman' on 29 May 2005.

For three summer seasons between 1985 and 1987, a former Buxton Class 104 DMU was specially painted and worked extra services between Crianlarich and Oban. Nicknamed 'The Mexican Bean', it is seen at Crianlarich on 5 September 1987.

The forerunner of the present day 'Royal Scotsman' was the 'Queen of Scots' set of coaches, photographed with 37422 in the yard at the former Crianlarich Lower station on 29 September 1988.

On 30 September 1988, I photographed only the second train that I saw at the former Crianlarich Lower station. 37412 had arrived with three empty fuel tanks from Oban and was about to add some loaded timber wagons to its train.

156457 in the National Express ScotRail livery passes Inverhaggernie, between Tyndrum and Crianlarich, with the mid-day Oban to Glasgow Queen Street service on 19 February 2003.

37402 rolls through Tyndrum Lower on 29 September 1988 with loaded fuel tanks for Oban and empty timber wagons that were to be left at Taynuilt.

37011 was approaching Tyndrum Lower with the Oban to Grangemouth empty fuel tanks on a cold early March day in the mid-1980s.

37406 was nearing Tyndrum Lower on a cold 29 October 1988 with the mid-day Oban to Glasgow Queen Street service.

156476 approaches Tyndrum Lower on 12 June 2021 with the 08.57 Oban to Glasgow Queen Street.

153305 and 156456 depart from Tyndrum Lower with the 10.34 Glasgow Queen Street to Oban on 28 August 2021.

B1 1264 runs towards Tyndrum Lower with an Oban to Springburn charter on 3 October 1999; the first time I have seen a steam locomotive with a set of deer antlers on the top lamp bracket over the smokebox door!

Class 31s 31190 and 31602 run down Glen Lochy on 29 May 2005, taking the 'Royal Scotsman' to Taynuilt.

156457 arrives at Dalmally on 12 June 2021 with the 12.15 from Oban to Glasgow Queen Street.

Class 156 156492 is arriving at the very photogenic station at Dalmally on 20 July 2021 with the 12.11 from Oban to Glasgow.

153373 and 156453 arrive at Dalmally on 20 July 2021 with the 10.34 from Glasgow Queen Street to Oban, passing 156492 on the 12.11 from Oban.

With Ben Lui as the backdrop, 156458 arrives at Dalmally on 20 July 2021 with the 12.23 from Glasgow Queen Street to Oban.

One of the most scenic locations on the Oban line is the Awe Viaduct to the west of Dalmally. On 30 September 1988, 37422 was crossing the viaduct with the mid-day Oban to Glasgow Queen Street service.

A pair of Fragonset Class 31s with 31602 leading 31601 cross the Awe Viaduct on 24 June 2000 with a Green Express railtour returning to Wigan from Oban.

West Coast Railways' 37248 leads DRS classmate 37688 across the Awe Viaduct on 5 May 2008 with a railtour returning to Newcastle from Oban.

B1 1264 crosses the Awe Viaduct in a very fortuitous patch of sunshine on an otherwise mostly cloudy day. 1264, complete with its set of antlers, was working an Oban to Springburn railtour on 3 October 1999.

156457 crosses the Awe Viaduct on 19 February 2003 with the 12.11 from Oban to Glasgow Queen Street.

156453 is in the ScotRail Saltire livery while 153373 is in the special livery advertising the West Highlands as they cross the Awe Viaduct on 20 July 2021 with the 14.41 from Oban to Glasgow Queen Street.

With D6817 leading D6851, the two Locomotive Services green Class 37s start to cross the Awe Viaduct on 12 June 2021 with the 13.50 Oban to Crewe charter.

156445 arrives at the very scenic station at Loch Awe on 29 April 2022 with the 08.22 Glasgow Queen Street to Oban.

156456 has stopped at the short platform at Falls of Cruachan on 29 April 2022 with the 08.57 from Oban to Glasgow Queen Street.

A year after the line to Oban opened, a train hit a landslide in the Pass of Brander and derailed. The secretary of the Callander and Oban Railway devised a system of wires running along the hillside linked to signals so that if a rock broke a wire, the signal would go to danger. There are now 17 signals along a stretch of track that is just over four miles in length and protected by posts with ten wires connected to the signals. This image shows one of the signals with two arms, one for each direction of travel.

156450 arrives at Taynuilt on 25 August 2021 with the 12.23 from Glasgow Queen Street to Oban.

D6851 and D6817 stop at Taynuilt to obtain a token for the section to Oban on 12 June 2021 with a 06.53 Carlisle to Oban charter.

156445 has arrived at Connel Ferry on 29 April 2022 with the 12.11 from Oban to Glasgow Queen Street. It is hard to visualise that this station used to have three platforms, a goods yard and a turntable to turn the engine that worked the branch to Ballachulish. The tracks into the adjacent fuel depot were removed earlier in 2022 after years of disuse, and the depot is now supplied by road.

37248 arrives at Oban on 5 May 2008 with a railtour from Newcastle. 37688 was uncoupled just before the station so that it could attach to the other end of the train in order to release 37248 from the bufferstops.

37248 has now coupled back in front of 37688 as the pair wait for departure time at Oban. In the distance, the Calmac ferry *The Clansman* is loading before departing for Craignure on the Isle of Mull.

156492 with 153377 wait at Oban on 25 August 2021, forming the 14.41 to Glasgow Queen Street.

Eastfield Depot's Class 25 25098 waits at the old Oban station before taking a train back to Glasgow Queen Street.

This was once Oban Station, and it was also a listed building. Repairs were needed, but no one was prepared to pay for them and so the building fell into disrepair and ended up having to be demolished.

A Scottish Railway Preservation Society (SRPS) railtour from Kirkcaldy is waiting time at Oban on 5 June 1976 with 27012 hauling a train of SRPS coaches that comprised its North British saloon, three ex-LMS Stanier coaches, two ex-Caledonian Railway coaches and the Great North of Scotland Railway's Royal Saloon!

Chapter 4
Crianlarich to Fort William

The West Highland Line leaves the station at Crianlarich and turns sharply to the east, traversing the valley on two short viaducts and a high embankment. It crosses over the main road and the site of the former Callander and Oban line before bridging the River Dochart. After reaching the eastern side, it curves sharply and starts to climb up the hillside towards Upper Tyndrum, five miles away, after which comes the final climb to County March Summit.

Upper Tyndrum was renamed from Tyndrum Upper when the RETB signalling was introduced. By keeping the station on the Oban line as Tyndrum Lower, having the West Highland station as Upper Tyndrum eliminated any confusion for the signalman at Banavie as to which station a train was at. As some services from Fort William combine at Crianlarich with a train from Oban, it is possible that the signalman at Banavie could receive calls from two trains, one at each of the stations at Tyndrum, at almost the same time so the renaming was the solution to eliminate any potential confusion.

Upper Tyndrum is one of the least used stations on the West Highland Line due to its location high on the hillside, and for passengers travelling towards Glasgow, there are only three ScotRail services a day whereas the station on the Oban line has six trains a day with two of them being almost at the same time. The RETB signalling between Helensburgh Upper and Upper Tyndrum became operational on 27 March 1988 and the second phase, from Upper Tyndrum to Fort William, was commissioned on 29 May 1988 after which the signal box was closed, and the station became unmanned.

After departing from Upper Tyndrum, trains have a stiff climb up to County March Summit at 1,024ft above sea level. After passing over the summit, the line runs along a ledge on the side of Beinn Odhar, a 2,948ft-high mountain. The builders of the West Highland Line were then faced with a problem; they needed to get the line to the other side of the valley but that would have meant the construction of a very high and long viaduct, which was unaffordable to them. The solution that was adopted is now known as 'The Horseshoe Curve', where the line descends on a steep gradient hugging the side of Beinn Odhar before curving very sharply round to cross the five-span Gleann Viaduct that takes the line onto the side of Beinn a'Chaiseil (2,897ft in height). It then curves further and crosses the nine-span Horseshoe Viaduct before arriving on the side of Beinn Dorain, a conical 3,524ft high mountain. The line has now arrived on the right side of the valley and in one mile has reduced height and curved through 180 degrees. The line now runs along the right-hand side of the valley before arriving at Bridge of Orchy.

Bridge of Orchy was opened on the day that the line was opened throughout to Fort William and has an engineers' siding on the north side. With the introduction of RETB signalling, it became another station where right hand running was adopted to make any shunting moves not have to handpump the sprung points. The station buildings are no longer just boarded up; they now enjoy a new lease of life as a bunkhouse for hikers travelling along the West Highland Way, a 96-mile walk over very rough terrain from Milngavie, just north of Glasgow, to Fort William. On average, 6,000 passengers a year use Bridge of Orchy station.

The West Highland Line leaves Bridge of Orchy and immediately starts the climb towards Rannoch Moor, one of Europe's last great wildernesses. For the next two miles, it climbs higher up the hillside until at Achallader, it curves round to the north and leaves the road to Glen Coe behind as it climbs up onto the moor. Halfway between Bridge of Orchy and Rannoch is the loop at Gorton. This is at an elevation of 1,100ft and has no road access. Before the introduction of RETB, there was a signal box here and a few cottages for the signalmen's families. Water, fuel and food was all brought in by train and an old railway carriage body served as a school. There was a short private platform for the use of railway staff and the people who lived at Gorton crossing.

Seven miles further on over the moor, the line reaches Rannoch station, which can also be reached by a narrow twisting road that starts over 40 miles away north of Pitlochry on the A9 Perth to Inverness road. The station building is now a famous tearoom offering an excellent variety of food, and Rannoch station is used each year by numerous walkers and cyclists. Rannoch station is one of the most remote in the UK; it is 18 miles from the nearest village of Kinloch Rannoch!

In order to build the line across the moor, which has large areas of bog land, the railway had to have the tracks laid on top of a mix of tree roots, branches, brushwood and earth. This added greatly to the cost of building the line, and when it reached Rannoch, there was a serious doubt that it would be able to go any further as the railway company building the line had run out of money. A director of both the West Highland Railway and the North British Railway was James Renton, and he was the line's salvation as he used a large portion of his personal fortune to ensure that the remainder of the railway would be built. In his honour, a group of railway navvies building the line brought a very large rock down from the moor and put it on the Fort William end of the platform. With their own tools, they carved a likeness of James Renton's head in the rock and the 'Renton Stone', as it is known, is still there today.

Seven miles across the moor from Rannoch and at a height of 1,340ft above sea level, the line reaches its summit at Corrour, which is the highest main line station in the UK. There is no public road access to Corrour, only a private track across the Corrour Estate. A mile from the station is a youth hostel at the head of Loch Ossian, and there is also accommodation available at and adjacent to the station. The area is very popular with walkers despite it being in such a remote area, Corrour station is the most used between Crianlarich and Fort William with an average number of just over 15,000 passengers using it each year.

The line leaves Corrour and soon starts a steep descent, which takes it to the east side of Loch Treig. On 28 June 2012, the North Blyth to Fort William train of alumina tanks hauled by GBRf's Class 66 66734 hit a landslide that had been caused by continuous very heavy rain. The locomotive derailed and slid down the bank, coming to a halt near the shore of the loch. The line was closed for around two weeks while repairs were made to the track and the hillside stabilised. The wagons that had remained upright were removed, but due to its remote location and the steepness of the terrain, it was not possible to recover 66734 so after parts that could be reused had been recovered, the locomotive was cut up on site by specialist contractors. About two miles from the next station at Tulloch, there was a temporary halt built at Fersit in the 1930s during the construction of the Lochaber hydro-electric scheme. After this work was completed, the platform was simply demolished and no trace of it now remains.

Tulloch is a two platform station in a very remote rural area. It has a siding on the north side of the line and the station buildings are now a hostel as the area is very popular with hikers and hill walkers. Between Tulloch and the next station at Roy Bridge, the line passes through the Monessie Gorge, a very narrow gorge with the line on a ledge high above the River Spean. There is a foot suspension bridge which allowed photographs of trains passing through the gorge but this was declared unsafe and closed after an inspection in 2021. The estate on whose lands it accessed is currently looking into how repairs can be made so that it can be reopened.

A short distance to the west is the station at Roy Bridge. This was once a two platform station with a passing loop with the station buildings on the north side platform. In 1966, the passing loop was taken out of use and removed, the former down platform was demolished as were the station buildings and all that remains now is a single platform with just a basic waiting shelter.

After a journey of just over three miles down the valley, the line arrives at Spean Bridge, a large village with a resident population of around 550 but with considerably more in the holiday season. Spean Bridge is a two-platform station but to enable easy shunting moves into the siding, right-hand running was adopted in 1987 when the RETB signalling was introduced. Like other stations along the line, the station buildings were designed by James Miller. In 1903, The Invergarry and Fort Augustus Railway opened and its passenger services ran from a bay platform on the north side of the station. This line was never profitable, and the passenger service was withdrawn in 1933, a victim of the rise of local bus services. The line continued to carry freight until 1947 when it was closed completely and all the tracks were lifted. The former station building is now a restaurant, and up to the start of the Covid pandemic, the station was used by around 8,000 passengers a year. Numbers fell when the travel restrictions were imposed but are now rapidly climbing back towards their former levels.

After Spean Bridge, the line travels for eight miles before reaching Fort William, first passing the aluminium smelter on the south side of the line. The complex has sidings that are used to hold the alumina tanks that travel up the West Highland Line either twice or three times a week from North Blyth. The smelter produces around 40,000 tons of aluminium a year in the form of 10-ton ingots, which are then sent south to be made into finished products. The ingots used to travel south by rail but now go south to the Central Belt of Scotland by road.

After passing the smelter, the line soon arrives at Fort William Junction where the line to Mallaig joins the West Highland Line and the junction signal box also controls access to Tom-na-Faire Depot. This depot is used all year round by ScotRail and between April and November by West Coast Railways, which operates the steam hauled 'Jacobite' tourist trains to Mallaig. The facility was opened in 1975 when the original depot was closed as part of the A82 road realignment and improvement scheme.

When the line was built, the signal box was called Banavie Junction as there was a branch line to the pier at Banavie to the west of Fort William. After the line to Mallaig was opened at the end of March 1901, it was renamed Mallaig Junction but to avoid any possible misunderstanding when the RETB signalling was introduced, it was renamed Fort William Junction.

A further half mile sees the line arrive at Fort William station. The original station was built 700 yards further west beside the pier, but to end huge delays to traffic on the old A82 road, a new road alignment alongside Loch Linne, which was to use part of the railway line, was planned, which meant that a new station had to be built. The last train to use the original station departed on 7 June 1975, and the station closed completely two days later and was then quickly demolished to make way for the new road construction. The new station was opened on 13 June 1975 and was refurbished with new showers and toilets in 2007 with the station building also housing a cafe. Colour light signals controlled from a panel in Fort William Junction signal box control all movements in and out of the station. The station has a ScotRail service of three trains each way to Glasgow and four each way to Mallaig. The Caledonian Sleeper runs six nights a week between Fort William and London and between April and November, the 'Jacobite' service runs daily with two trains a day at peak season.

The Class 67s took over hauling the Fort William sleeper from 11 June 2006. On one of the very last times a Class 37 was used on a West Highland sleeper train, 37401 arrives at Crianlarich with the working from London Euston on 8 June 2006.

156493 and 156477 approach Crianlarich on 8 April 2019 with the 10.10 from Mallaig to Glasgow Queen Street.

37413 and 37419 arrive at Crianlarich on 5 April 2000 with the daily Fort William to Mossend freight.

A Class 156 crosses the A85 road and will shortly arrive at Crianlarich station on 20 July 2021 with a train from Mallaig to Glasgow Queen Street.

66105 is crossing over the River Dochart as it leaves Crianlarich with the North Blyth to Fort William alumina tanks on 3 May 2008.

Tyndrum Upper, which is now Upper Tyndrum, is a typical West Highland station with an island platform and similar station buildings, photographed from the cab of a northbound Class 37 shortly before the introduction of the RETB signalling.

66737 climbs the last few yards into Upper Tyndrum with the loaded alumina tanks from North Blyth to Fort William on 21 April 2022.

One common feature of many of the West Highland stations was that access to the platform was via an entry that took passengers under one of the running lines to a flight of stairs. 66737 waits at Upper Tyndrum over the entrance to the station on 21 April 2022 to obtain the RETB token to Bridge of Orchy from the signalling centre at Banavie.

66105 is climbing from Upper Tyndrum to County March Summit on 3 May 2008 when EWS still had the contract to work the alumina trains between North Blyth and Fort William.

In the First Group ScotRail livery, 156457 climbs towards County March on 5 May 2008 with the 08.23 Glasgow Queen Street to Mallaig.

37406 was slowly climbing the last half mile to County March Summit with a loaded ballast train, the 08.38 from Millerhill to Fort William, on 6 March 2006.

66737 climbs up to County March Summit with the loaded alumina tanks from North Blyth to Fort William on 21 April 2022.

37197 and 37261 'top and tail' the 'Royal Scotsman' on the climb up to County March Summit on 6 August 2005 with the Edinburgh to Spean Bridge leg of a three-night 'Western' tour.

37406 was working the Euston to Fort William sleeper from Edinburgh on 17 September 2003 and had almost reached the top of the climb up to County March Summit.

The shape of things to come. 67004 climbs up to County March on a trial sleeper run on 4 October 2003 from Polmadie to Fort William.

57314 has reached the summit at County March with a 09.53 Edinburgh to Rannoch 'Northern Belle' outing. 47854 was on the rear and giving the train a push up to the summit on 28 August 2021.

37606 passes County March on 5 April 2000 with the Fort William to Coatbridge aluminium ingots; the conical Beinn Dorain at 3,524ft makes a stunning backdrop.

37667 and 37410 pass County March with a SRPS railtour returning from Mallaig and Fort William to Ayr on 22 May 2004.

37419 approaches County March Summit on 16 June 2000 with the empty Alcan tanks from Fort William to North Blyth.

On the very cold wintry day of 5 March 2000 in a period of torrential rain at County March, Deltic 55019 came south from Fort William with a charter returning to Cardiff.

On 6 August 2005, the SRPS railtour from Dundee to Mallaig and return became the first excursion working on the West Highland Line to be hauled by Class 47 locomotives. In the evening, 47826 passes County March with the return leg to Dundee.

156499 and 156493 pass County March Summit on their way south with the 10.10 from Mallaig to Glasgow Queen Street on 28 August 2021.

As the line descends into the Horseshoe, it curves to the right and drops down before a very tight turn to the left takes it over Gleann Viaduct, the first of the two viaducts at the Horseshoe. This was the view from the cab of a Class 37 that I was travelling in looking down at Gleann Viaduct.

On 8 April 2019, 'The Statesman' ran south from Fort William to Peterborough with 47593 leading and 47501 on the rear and were photographed as the train crossed the nine-span Horseshoe Viaduct.

Dwarfed by the mountains, 66737 runs along the base of Beinn Dorain at Auch, between The Horseshoe and Bridge of Orchy, with the loaded alumina tanks from North Blyth to Fort William.

On 4 October 2003, B1 61264 disguised as former classmate 61244 *Strang Steel* waits at Bridge of Orchy for the arrival of a northbound Class 156 before it can depart to Upper Tyndrum.

On 6 April 2004, 66106 was departing from Bridge of Orchy with a Mossend to Fort William freight that, as well as the 11 loaded Alcan tanks, also conveyed four loaded china clay tanks for the paper mill at Corpach.

31190 and 37261 climb away from Bridge of Orchy with an Edinburgh Waverley to Spean Bridge leg of a 'Royal Scotsman' three-night 'Western' tour on 14 May 2005.

37406 thrashes away from Bridge of Orchy on 6 March 2006 with the 08.38 Millerhill to Fort William loaded ballast.

Class 31 31190 and BR Standard Class 4 75014 climb past Achallader and head towards Rannoch Moor on 16 June 2000 with empty stock for use on the steam-hauled services between Fort William and Mallaig.

66737 arrives at the remote station at Rannoch on 7 March 2022 with the 08.07 Fort William to North Blyth empty alumina tanks, passing the 'Renton Stone' at the north end of the platform.

156476 calls at Rannoch on 7 March 2022 with the 10.10 from Mallaig to Glasgow Queen Street.

With 47614 leading and 47593 on the rear, 'The Statesman' from Fort William to Stevenage departs from Rannoch on 7 March 2022 after a stop that let the passengers alight to admire the scenery while the train waited for a northbound DMU to arrive and clear the section to Bridge of Orchy.

A private Locomotive Services charter arrives at Rannoch on 7 March 2022 behind a pair of green Class 37s wearing their original BR numbers of D6817 and D6851.

There were only three tall brick-built signal boxes on the West Highland Line; at Glen Douglas, Gorton and Corrour with all the others being built on station platforms. With no public roads to Corrour, this had to be a shot from a passing train and it was taken on 5 May 1979 from a Dundee to Mallaig SRPS railtour when the train had stopped at Corrour for a tablet exchange. A Class 27 was waiting with a southbound freight to access the line to Rannoch.

156500 and 156477 arrive at Spean Bridge on 3 September 2021 with the 10.10 Mallaig to Glasgow Queen Street. The track to the west looked in urgent need of a visit from a weedkilling train!

37667 and 37410 are about to pass the Fort William smelter on 22 May 2004 with a SRPS railtour returning from Mallaig to Ayr.

66741 and 73967 pass Fort William Junction signal box on 3 September 2021 with the overnight Caledonian Sleeper from London Euston.

On 2 September 2021, 66741 and 73967 depart from Fort William with the Caledonian Sleeper to London Euston.

156477 and 156500 arrive at Fort William on 2 September 2021 with the 18.15 from Mallaig.

Chapter 5
The Mallaig Extension

Many people refer to the Fort William to Mallaig line as part of the West Highland Line, but that is not its correct name, it should be called The Mallaig Extension. When the West Highland Line arrived at Fort William, it was recognised that although Fort William was on the west coast, it was too far from the fishing grounds and that getting there involved too long a voyage. The solution was to build a railway that would link Fort William with the village of Mallaig. The proposal to build the line received Royal Assent on 31 July 1894 and the line was opened to traffic on 1 April 1901.

The contractor used to build the line was Robert McAlpine and Sons and due to his extensive use of concrete in the building of the railway, it earned him the nickname of 'Concrete Bob'. When the line was being constructed, much of it was in very difficult terrain, and the local stone was incredibly hard to quarry so that is why use was made of concrete. The line is renowned for the many concrete structures it has with perhaps the best known being the 21-arch Glenfinnan Viaduct, which is now recognised around the world since appearing in the Harry Potter films.

The line turns off to the west at Fort William Junction and soon crosses the River Lochy on a girder bridge before arriving at Banavie, which is a single platform station. At its west end is the RETB Banavie Signalling Centre, designed to look like a large signal box, and it is situated alongside the swing bridge over the Caledonian Canal, which it also controls. A feature of the canal is that after the swing bridges under the railway and then the road to Mallaig, the canal climbs 62 feet in a quarter of a mile in a series of eight locks. This staircase lock known as Neptune's Staircase was built by the renowned canal engineer Thomas Telford between 1803 and 1822.

After passing Banavie, the line runs past Corpach another single platform station and then passes the timber works where the sidings used to be worked from Annat signal box. After that, the line continues westwards along the north side of Loch Eil and passes the single platform at Loch Eil Outward Bound, which is also a RETB token point. After that, it runs in a fairly straight line until after the end of the loch, it then starts to climb, passing through a short tunnel before slowing to cross the curving Glenfinnan Viaduct, which offers a superb view of the head of Loch Sheil. The line then arrives at Glenfinnan station, which has two platforms and a passing loop, the first one on the line since leaving Fort William. The station buildings at Glenfinnan are now a railway museum and the adjacent signal box has also been preserved.

As the railway leaves Glenfinnan, it climbs steeply and reaches the summit on the line at Lech-a-Vuie at 379ft above sea level. At one time, there was a private platform here for shooting parties on the Inverailort Estate. The line then descends and runs on the south side of Loch Eilt. After passing the head of the loch, the line curves sharply in an 'S' curve, running under the road and after that it soon arrives at Lochailort station. This was once a double platform station with a passing loop but the loop and the platform on the north side were taken out of use in 1966 and the loop was subsequently removed. After the station became unmanned, the station buildings fell into disrepair and became badly damaged, resulting in them being demolished in the mid-1970s.

The line passes the well-known photographic location of Polnish and then climbs to pass Loch Dubh before descending to Loch nan Uamh Viaduct. It was near here that Bonnie Prince Charlie landed at the start of his campaign to take over the British throne in the Jacobite uprising of 1745. When the line was being constructed, it was rumoured that a horse and cart fell inside the main central pier; recent x-rays have confirmed that its skeleton is there and that the story is indeed a true one. After passing through the tunnel at the west end of the viaduct, the line starts to climb the short but steep Beasdale Bank. There are three more short tunnels and some sharp curves on the mile and a half 1 in 48 climb before the summit is reached at Beasdale station, which has just a single platform and it was not until 1965 that it was opened to the public. It was built as a private station for the use of people using the nearby Arisaig House. When the Covid pandemic struck, Beasdale was one of only six stations in the UK that had no passengers at all for over a year! The station house has been converted into a holiday home.

After Beasdale, the line continues to Arisaig, the most westerly station in the UK mainland, but before it gets there, it crosses Borrodale Bridge. At one time, the bridge with the longest single concrete span in the world at 127ft 6in. Arisaig is a two-platform station and is the second passing loop on the line. The station is uphill on the north side of the village, which has a population of just over 300 residents and an average number of passengers using the station of 6,000. The line then turns north and descends to pass over and around Keppoch Moss, which caused problems during the line's construction, before it again climbs a short distance and arrives at Morar, another single platform station.

After Morar, the line descends and for the last two miles to Mallaig, it runs alongside the sea, giving passengers great views of the Inner Hebridean islands of Eigg, Rum and Canna. Before the railway reached Mallaig, it was just a small fishing village but in the ten years after the railway arrived, the village expanded and Mallaig became a major fishing port with many fish trains using the line to take the valuable commodity to the markets of Central Scotland. It is still a ferry port as Calmac operates a ferry service from Mallaig to Armadale on Skye and to the small isles, but the line's main traffic nowadays is tourist traffic.

The old Fort William station with a pair of Class 24s on a charter from Edinburgh and a pair of Class 27s on the other end waiting to take the train to Mallaig.

26037 waits at Fort William with a train to Mallaig on 16 August 1980 as two of the SRPS' vintage coaches are stabled in the adjacent siding; a LNER Gresley buffet and an ex-LMS Stanier Third Open.

37404 waits for departure time at Fort William with a train for Glasgow Queen Street on 24 September 1987.

Black Five 45212 passes the disused fuel depot at Fort William on 3 September 2021 with the 10.15 'Jacobite' to Mallaig.

156457 and 156456 run on a completely new length of track that was re-laid in March 2022 as they leave Fort William for Glasgow Queen Street on 29 April 2022.

73971 and 73969 are in the process of running from where they had been stabled in the former fuel depot to Fort William station on 29 April 2022 to collect the Caledonian Sleeper coaches and shunt them into the platform ready for their evening departure to London Euston.

Right: With 47854 leading and 47826 on the rear, a SRPS charter is approaching Fort William Yard on 6 August 2005, returning to Fort William from Mallaig.

Below: A BR Standard 4 2-6-0, 76079, which had been renumbered as 76001, crosses the Lochy Viaduct as it left Fort William for Mallaig on 22 May 2004.

156457 departs from Banavie for Fort William with Ben Nevis, the UK's highest mountain at 4,413ft above sea level, as the backdrop.

156450 and 156457 arrive at Banavie on 29 April 2022, passing the Banavie RETB signalling centre, with the 16.01 from Mallaig to Glasgow Queen Street.

Stanier 2-8-0 48151 was an unusual visitor to the Mallaig line in the summer off 1999. On 1 August, it is seen leaving Corpach with the 10.15 Fort William to Mallaig.

156500 and 156477 approach Loch Eil Outward Bound on 29 April 2022 with the 12.23 Glasgow Queen Street to Mallaig.

37423 runs alongside Loch Eil at Fassfern with a Fort William to Mallaig service on 29 September 1988.

Black Five 5407 slowly crosses Glenfinnan Viaduct with a Fort William to Mallaig working in August 1984.

48151 is climbing the last few yards to Glenfinnan station on 1 August 1999 with the 10.15 'The Jacobite' from Fort William to Mallaig.

76001 arrives at Glenfinnan with the Fort William to Mallaig steam service on 22 May 2004.

With 37667 leading and 37410 on the rear, a SRPS railtour returning to Ayr on 22 May 2004 was approaching Glenfinnan station.

45212 climbs away from Glenfinnan with the morning 'Jacobite', the 10.15 from Fort William to Mallaig, on 2 September 2021.

5407 powers through Lochailort in August 1984 with the 10.15 steam service from Fort William to Mallaig, at that time called the 'West Highlander'.

K1 2005 climbs past Polnish with the 'The Jacobite' from Fort William to Mallaig on 28 June 1988.

37423 in its Railfreight sub-sector livery passes the little chapel at Polnish on 29 September 1988 with a Fort William to Mallaig service.

After seemingly being abandoned for several years, the former chapel at Polnish is now a private residence. On 1 September 2021, 156446 and 156456 pass by with the 12.23 Glasgow Queen Street to Mallaig.

47826 climbs between Polnish and Loch nan Uamh on 6 August 2005 with a Dundee to Mallaig SRPS railtour. This was the first time a Class 47 had ever worked a train from Fort William to Mallaig.

37409 crosses Loch nan Uamh Viaduct on 5 September 1987 with a Fort William to Mallaig service.

Left: 47854 has just crossed Loch nan Uamh Viaduct on 6 August 2005 with the SRPS railtour returning from Mallaig to Dundee.

Below: Black Five 44871 bursts out of the tunnel and onto Loch nan Uamh Viaduct with the afternoon 'Jacobite' returning to Fort William on 1 September 2021.

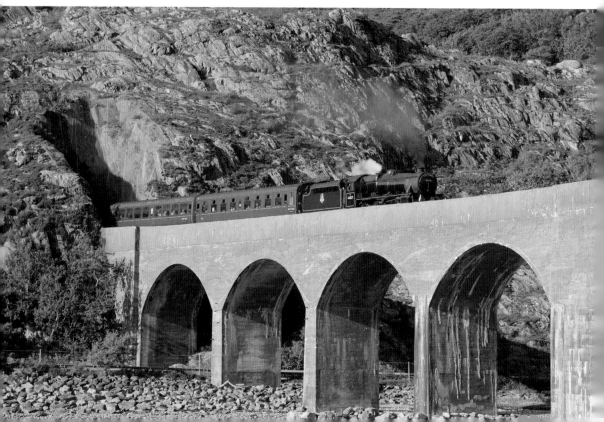

156493 and 156474 cross Loch nan Uamh Viaduct on 1 September 2021 with the 16.01 Mallaig to Glasgow Queen Street.

156474 and 156493 approach Arisaig on 1 September 2021 with the 08.23 from Glasgow Queen Street to Mallaig.

37404 makes a rousing start from Arisaig on 5 September 1987 with a service from Mallaig to Fort William.

76001 with the Mallaig to Fort William steam service crosses the SRPS railtour from Ayr to Mallaig, with Class 37 37667 on the rear, at Arisaig on 22 May 2004.

Arisaig is normally a very quiet rural station on the Mallaig line. On 12 May 1984, it had a very large number of people on the platform who were travelling on the F&W Tours 'Skirl o' the Pipes 4' railtour hauled by 37022, which was waiting for a train from Mallaig to arrive before it could access the single line.

156493 and 156492 arrive at Morar on 2 September 2021 with the 08.23 from Glasgow Queen Street to Mallaig.

37410 was photographed between Morar and Mallaig on 22 May 2004 with the SRPS railtour from Ayr to Mallaig.

76001 rests at Mallaig before returning to Fort William on 22 May 2004. The Inner Hebridean islands of Rum and Eigg can be seen in the distance.

The railway scene at Mallaig has certainly changed since this view was taken on 12 May 1984. 37022 is running round its train while the secondman is sitting on the rail waiting to couple the loco back onto its train with not a high-vis vest to be seen. In the background, a sheep can be seen grazing beside the tracks with others hidden behind the coaches! 37022 would depart later for Fort William and after running round there, would then take the train south to Glasgow.

156493 and 156492 rest at the terminus at Mallaig on 2 September 2021 before working the 16.01 to Glasgow Queen Street.

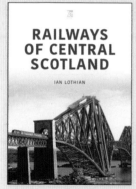
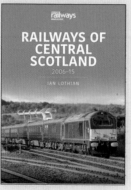
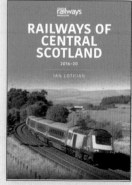
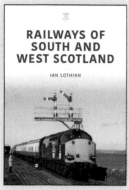
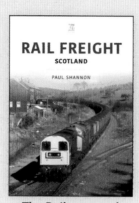
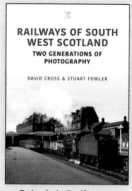